Original title:
Why Life Is a Joke (And I'm Not in On It)

Copyright © 2025 Creative Arts Management OÜ
All rights reserved.

Author: Kieran Blackwood
ISBN HARDBACK: 978-1-80566-083-5
ISBN PAPERBACK: 978-1-80566-378-2

Whispering Punchlines at Midnight

In shadows soft, the giggles creep,
As clocks tick-tock, secrets we keep.
With whispers loud, we share our woes,
In punchline dreams, absurdity grows.

The moonlight dances, chuckles abound,
While reason hides, nowhere to be found.
Each star a jest, each cloud a tease,
In midnight's air, we laugh with ease.

The Laughter Between Heartbeats

Tickle my soul with a giggling breeze,
Between each heart's beat, humor's keys.
Life's a riddle wrapped in a grin,
A chorus of chuckles where we begin.

We trip on shoes of mismatched size,
Uproarious moments wrapped in disguise.
Every misstep a laugh on the road,
In the heart of chaos, joy's seeds are sowed.

Trapped in a Comedy Sketch

Stuck on this stage, lights shining bright,
Each scripted line a humorous plight.
With wooden props and a ghostly crew,
We play our part, though none have a clue.

The audience snickers, they can't get enough,
Of clumsy falls and whimsical stuff.
With every take, the laughter flows,
In this sketch of life, anything goes.

Delusions of the Scripted Life

Life's a scene with no clear intent,
A sitcom world where logic is bent.
Each day a chapter of slapstick cheer,
With punchlines hiding, always near.

Our heads shake in bemusement, it's true,
As our dreams take flight, like a wayward zoo.
With every mistake, we find the delight,
In scripted tomorrows, we laugh through the night.

The Humor in Humiliation

I tripped on air, fell on my face,
The world just laughed, no saving grace.
My dignity's lost, but here's the twist,
In my own blunder, I can't resist.

Strangers giggle, they snicker and tease,
I wear the embarrassment like a warm breeze.
A slip on the ice, my flailing limbs,
The audience roars; my laughter begins.

I ask myself, 'Is this a cruel fate?'
Yet amidst the chaos, I celebrate.
For every mishap, a story's spun,
The punchline's revealed, and I'm still having fun.

So let the world chuckle at my expense,
In the circus of life, I find recompense.
With each stumble and fall, a lesson new,
The humor in humbling, forever shines through.

Chuckling in the Wind's Embrace

The wind whispers jokes as it tousles my hair,
I laugh like a fool, without any care.
Clouds join the fun, their shapes bend and sway,
Painting the sky in a whimsical display.

I met a squirrel, with acorns galore,
He stared right at me; I laughed even more.
His mischief was clear, with antics so bold,
As he danced on a branch, a sight to behold.

Life's sense of humor is crazy and wild,
It tickles the senses like a playful child.
In every mishap, a giggle is found,
In every stumble, a chuckle unbound.

So here in the moment, I find pure delight,
In the joy of the journey, the laughs in the night.
With the wind as my partner, I'll take on the world,
In this game of life, let the humor unfurl.

Jester's Lament

I wear a grin, my heart in chains,
The punchlines land, but bring me pains.
A court of laughter, I'm the fool,
In jest and jibe, I'm just the tool.

Life's a stage, a comedic farce,
With script unwritten, nothing's sparse.
The world laughs loud, as I slip and fall,
In every giggle, a silent call.

Life's Pranks Amidst the Serious

In suits and ties, we tread the line,
But humor hides in dollar signs.
With every sigh, the cosmos winks,
While sanity teeters on the brink.

A banana peel lays in the gloom,
I trip and tumble, sealed my doom.
Yet here I stand with a snicker's breath,
Dancing through life, I jest with death.

Droll Moments in Despair

A serious face in a silly place,
Where laughter echoes, a warm embrace.
With every frown, a punchline's due,
I chuckle softer, what else to do?

Life's a riddle wrapped in jest,
While I stumble, it's surely blessed.
In darkened corners, the giggles creep,
For humor grows where the sorrows seep.

The Misguided Muse of Comedy

I chased a dream, it turned to jest,
The muse I sought, gave me no rest.
With every laugh, a tear resides,
In humor's arms, my heart confides.

I juggle woes like fragile glass,
As irony watches, with a sly laugh.
Yet here I am, in awkward glee,
A jester's soul, both wild and free.

Mirth in the Face of Misfortune

In the middle of a stormy day,
My umbrella flew far away.
I danced in puddles, splashed around,
Laughing loud, joy abounds.

A cat crossed my path, not a care,
Whiskers twitching in the air.
I tripped right over a pile of leaves,
The world's a stage, with silly thieves.

A sudden sneeze, the skies turned gray,
The clouds rolled in to ruin my play.
But with each drop that splashed my face,
I grinned at the sky, embraced the grace.

Life throws pies, but I'll not fret,
Jokes and jests, the best are met.
In every twist, a chuckle blooms,
Humor brightens all the glooms.

Uninvited Giggles

I walked into a room of frowns,
Where whispers echoed all around.
Till someone slipped on a banana peel,
Laughter burst, it felt surreal.

A serious meeting turned to fun,
When the office chair began to run.
Round and round at dizzying speed,
Office life, a comic breed.

With every glance, the humor grows,
Life's a canvas, filled with prose.
In missteps and slips, we find delight,
Giggles arise in the midst of night.

The calendar's filled with daunting tasks,
Yet still, we wear our jester masks.
In the uninvited giggles we share,
Is the secret to raise the air.

Clowns in the Mirror

Mirror, mirror, what do you see?
A clown with a goofy hat, oh me!
With a red nose and painted face,
Reflecting joys, a silly space.

Behind the glass, reality's bent,
Each grimace made, a laugh is sent.
I trip on thoughts and tumble down,
In this reflection, I wear the crown.

Life's a circus, full of tricks,
With every stumble, humor mixes.
A pratfall here, a juggling act,
In the mirror's glow, we're intact.

So laugh with me at every blunder,
In the funhouse, there's no thunder.
Clowns in the mirror, what a sight,
In this carnival, we feel so light.

A Play Where I'm Not the Star

The curtain rises, I take my seat,
Watching others dance to the beat.
With scripts in hand, they steal the show,
I chuckle quietly, enjoying the flow.

The lead forgets lines, stumbles on cue,
The audience giggles at all that he'll do.
I sit back, sipping popcorn with glee,
Life's a theater, come dance with me.

Roles are shuffled, a brand-new plot,
Each scene a twist, hasn't life forgot?
I'm the silent witness to the play,
In fits of laughter, I drift away.

Though not the star, I feel the thrill,
As fun unfolds, I get my fill.
In this grand show with its wheezing clowns,
I embrace joy in the ups and downs.

Tumbling Through the Jokey Maze

In a world that's upside down,
I trip over my own shoes.
Laughter hides in every frown,
Guess it's just the daily news.

A banana peel beneath my feet,
I slide into a goofy fall.
People laugh, it's such a treat,
Life's a stage, and I'm the fool.

The more I scream, the more they cheer,
Punchlines fly like confetti.
I'll tell a joke but no one's near,
Does this mean my humor's petty?

In this maze where giggles reign,
I'm lost but hey, that's all right.
I trip again, a hint of pain,
Yet laughter turns it into light.

Laughter in the Silence of Suffering

With a frown that breaks the rules,
I juggle sorrows on a whim.
Life's a dance of clumsy fools,
And I'm just here on a limb.

Muffled giggles drown my cries,
As I slip on joy's embrace.
Strange how chaos wears a disguise,
That brings a smile to my face.

When the clouds roll in with doubt,
I crack a joke, it's plain to see.
Laughter bubbles, wipes it out,
A strange sort of remedy.

In the quiet, chuckles bloom,
A paradox that feels so right.
Suffering drapes its darkened room,
Yet humor spills like stars at night.

The Comedian Who Lost His Script

On the stage, I stand alone,
My lines have flown, not one in sight.
Laughter echoes through the tone,
As I fumble in the spotlight.

A one-liner slipped from my grasp,
The punchline danced right out the door.
I smile wide and take a rasp,
Forgetting what I came here for.

The crowd still laughs, I drop my veil,
They find it funny, my despair.
In this chaos, I prevail,
Guess no one minds the lack of care.

With every stumble, cheers arise,
My obvious flaws bring such delight.
Who needs a script when laughter flies?
I'll bask in joy with all my might.

In Jest, We Scream

Amid the chaos of it all,
I find a quirky, silly sound.
When life delivers its hardball,
I laugh and throw my woes around.

In jest, we dance with our own fears,
A tangled web of jests and pain.
Soft chuckles help dissolve the tears,
And lighten up this silly game.

With every blunder, joy will sprout,
Like daisies sprinking dirt with glee.
Screaming laughter shouts in doubt,
A remedy we all agree.

So here's to joy and silly schemes,
For life can twist in odd embrace.
In jest, we scream, fulfill our dreams,
Finding humor in the race.

The Cosmic Punchline

The stars above are giggling,
While we dance like fools below.
The universe has a chuckle,
As we juggle dreams and woe.

Reality plays tricks on us,
Like a cat with a ball of yarn.
We chase it round, laugh it off,
Who knew this could cause such harm?

Echoes of laughter haunts the night,
As we ponder life's great riddle.
Is it all a grand setup,
Or just us twirling in the middle?

So let's toast to cosmic humor,
With wine that tastes just like rain.
For in this circus of existence,
We'll wear our clown shoes with no shame.

Laughing Through the Tears

The world spins, a dizzy show,
With laughter laced in every sigh.
We juggle joy and tragedy,
While wearing smiles with a lie.

With each slip on life's banana peel,
We find a chuckle, then a groan.
The path is strewn with funny slips,
Yet we walk it all alone.

Tears can be such silly things,
Like rain on a cloudless day.
But even as they tumble down,
We laugh the pain away.

So let's embrace this wild ride,
With humor as our trusty guide.
For deep inside this twisted maze,
A chuckle's waiting right outside.

The Absurdity of Being

We're all just clowns in this big top,
Playing roles in a grand charade.
Ducking pies and slipping on floors,
While laughing at the mess we've made.

Existence is a jumbled act,
Punchlines sneaking up behind.
The universe writes our script,
But the humor's hard to find.

We stumble over life's logic,
And question what we think we know.
Is it a game or a riddle?
In a comedy, the plot won't flow.

Yet we play on with hearts wide open,
Turning sorrow to a jest.
In absurdity, we find our laughter,
And wear hilarity like a vest.

Tumbleweeds of Time

Time rolls by like tumbleweeds,
Bouncing off our anxious lives.
We chase each joke the moment brings,
While confusion always thrives.

With every tick, a prankster's grin,
As minutes turn to fleeting bliss.
We stumble through this spoof of time,
And wonder what we might have missed.

Like jesters in a crowded court,
We slip and slide, unsure of ground.
But every laugh that breaks the silence,
Turns the chaos into sound.

So here's to days that feel absurd,
With punchlines lurking at each turn.
For in the mayhem, we'll find joy,
And with each giggle, let it burn.

Witty Remarks from the Universe

Stars twinkle like they're laughing,
While planets spin in silly prancing.
Comets race with vivid trails,
Echoing giggles in cosmic gales.

Earth's got a sense of humor, too,
With clouds that puffy and bow like they coo.
Rain falls like tears from grinning skies,
As puddles form with joyful sighs.

Birds chirp jokes in playful flight,
Squirrels act cute, what a delight!
Every tumble, every fall,
Life's slapstick, a comedic sprawl.

In this show, I play my part,
With jokes tossed around like a dart.
Yet here I stand, not quite in on,
The punchlines missed, I smile and yawn.

The Joke's on the Unaware

Life's a riddle wrapped in jest,
A treasure hunt, a funny quest.
But I'm the one who's lost the key,
While laughter rings, it's never me.

The clocks tick to the beat of glee,
Yet I seem stuck on one, you see.
Friends roll in laughter, tears they share,
While I'm left dodging life's wild glare.

Puns scatter like leaves in the breeze,
While I scratch my head, unable to tease.
Inside jokes weaved with gleeful flair,
I chuckle along, though unaware.

But here's the twist, oh what a thrill,
Life's punchlines strike like a well-aimed quill.
Each stumble's comedic, a slapstick feat,
As I trip over laughs laid at my feet.

Intermission in the Comedy of Life

Curtains down, let's take a stroll,
In a world where humor takes its toll.
Every mishap, a scene so rich,
Like slapstick films that flicker and twitch.

People dance with a clumsy grace,
While I'm just trying to find my place.
Every chuckle feels like a trap,
As I sit back, just catch the flap.

Falling cakes and snoozing cats,
A world draped in pratfalls and chats.
I sip my drink, a funny sight,
As sarcasm drips from day to night.

So here I sit, amidst the cheer,
Jokes whizz past, but never near.
Taking a break from this lively show,
Where humor flows, but I don't know.

Caught in the Punchline

I stepped on stage, but missed my cue,
While laughter soared, I just withdrew.
The spotlight shines, but not on me,
As punchlines land like a bumblebee.

Clowns juggle time, with flair they twist,
While I trip over an unseen mist.
The audience rolls, what a parade,
And I'm the one who's been misplayed.

Life throws pies, a soft surrender,
While I'm left holding the poor blender.
The gags fly high, a dizzying spin,
And I'm just grinning, caught in the din.

With every fall, I laugh at fate,
Knowing I've shown up a bit too late.
But in this wild, comedic spree,
I find my joy, however zany it be.

Winks from the Cosmos

Stars giggle in the night,
Planets spin with delight.
Comets trail silly dreams,
While the universe teems.

Galaxies leap and dance,
In a cosmic, wild prance.
Black holes pull us with glee,
What a strange jubilee!

Alien faces in flight,
Waving with all their might.
Lights flicker, oh so bright,
Is this all just for fright?

Cosmic jesters on parade,
In this grand charade.
We laugh till we expire,
Under the universe's fire.

The Ridiculousness of Routine

Coffee spills on the floor,
As I rush out the door.
Toast pops up all burnt,
I feel slightly churned.

Mirrors reflect with a grin,
As I try to tuck in.
Socks mismatched, hair askew,
What a hilarious view!

At work, I trip on my shoe,
While laughing at my crew.
Meetings filled with strange plays,
Time just slips away.

The clock ticks but it's wrong,
Life's a never-ending song.
Gags in every mundane,
Routine never feels plain.

Farcical Fables of Existence

Once a cat wore a crown,
Thought it ruled the whole town.
Chased its tail for a quest,
What a royal jest!

A dog barked at the moon,
Singing a silly tune.
"Why so bright?" he would yell,
In this odd, doggy spell.

Fish who dream of the sky,
Wishing they all could fly.
Bubbles burst in a cheer,
As the clouds all appeared.

Chickens plot with a wink,
"Let's escape with a blink!"
In tales where laughter is king,
Life's a comical fling.

Laughter in the Shadows

In the corner, giggles peek,
Making the strong-hearted weak.
Whispers dance like the breeze,
"Don't take life with such ease!"

Monsters hide with a chuckle,
As they plan for a shuffle.
Frights turn into a jest,
As they play with the best.

Shadows skip down the hall,
While I stumble and fall.
Echoes bounce with a cheer,
Every giggle draws near.

Underneath the starlit sky,
All the worries pass by.
In this corner so bright,
Laughter conquers the night.

Jokes That Slice Deep

In the mirror I see a clown,
With a frown and a big red nose,
I trip on life's banana peel,
And laugh at where the path goes.

Every punchline lands like a stone,
Yet I chuckle at the pain,
Life's a joke with a bitter twist,
And I'm left to entertain.

Friends all giggle at my plight,
While I'm wrapped in silent dread,
Like a jester without a court,
Playing with words I never said.

But here's the punchline, if you please,
We're all part of this messy play,
Take a bow and take the fall,
Life's a punchline, come what may.

Laughing at My Own Expense

I bought a ticket to my life,
But it's a show with no one there,
The stage is set, the lights are dim,
Yet I act like I don't care.

With every joke that flops and fails,
I learn to laugh from my mistakes,
The audience? Just my own two feet,
As I trip on all the stakes.

I serve the punchlines with a grin,
Even when they cut me deep,
With humor's light, I wear my scars,
In this circus, I don't sleep.

So here's a toast with empty cups,
To the jesters of the day,
We stumble through this wild rigmarole,
Together, we'll find our way.

The Trickster I've Yet to Meet

There's a trickster hiding in the crowd,
With a wink and a knowing grin,
I search for them in every face,
But I'm the fool who wears the skin.

Their laughter echoes through the air,
As I juggle my own mistakes,
Like a magician with no audience,
I laugh off the risks it takes.

The punchlines come but never land,
Like confetti blown by the breeze,
I chase the jester I can't find,
While life plays poker with my knees.

But the trickster's map is drawn in quirks,
Leading me to a laugh-filled fate,
In every stumble, every chance,
I celebrate as I create.

Insanity Wrapped in Humor

Insanity sits across the room,
Dressed in polka dots and charm,
It tugs at me with feigned surprise,
Saying life will do no harm.

We roll the dice and spin the wheel,
In this game of merry fate,
I'm the joker chuckling loud,
As chaos serves, I contemplate.

With a punchline that never fits,
I laugh until I'm out of breath,
Juggling woes and silly dreams,
Even in the face of death.

Yet here I am, all wrapped in jest,
Finding joy in every wrong,
In this twisted, funny play,
I'll sing my madcap song.

Giggles at the Edge of Sorrow

In a world where shadows play,
The sun forgets to greet the day.
Laughter bubbles, yet feels so strange,
As dreams and punchlines rearrange.

Jesters dance with heavy hearts,
While smiles wear their worn-out parts.
We trip on joy, fall into frowns,
Life spins, but who wears the crowns?

Through chaos, chuckles softly creep,
In this comedy, we laugh, we weep.
With every joke, a truth is tossed,
In jest, we find the lines we crossed.

Yet here we stand, a merry band,
Spinning tales, hand in hand.
For every sigh, a giggle's glow,
In laughter's arms, we learn to flow.

Whispers of a Comedian's Regret

In crowded rooms, the silence sings,
As laughter hides behind its strings.
A punchline quivers in the air,
Yet no one hears the hidden care.

The mic is hot, but so's my brow,
Cracking jokes, but lost somehow.
Falling flat on dreams of mirth,
These jests, they travel 'round the Earth.

Behind the scenes, a veil of tears,
What's funny echoes into fears.
The crowd erupts, I hold a sigh,
For every laugh, a quiet why.

With every giggle, a heart may break,
Lost in laughter, for laughter's sake.
Yet in the chaos, spirits mend,
Mirth's shadow dances, never ends.

Chasing a Punchline that Never Arrives

I tell a joke, it drifts away,
Like socks in laundry, gone astray.
The clock ticks loudly, laughter stalls,
Tickled dreams behind the walls.

In pursuit of giggles, I miss the mark,
Chasing shadows in the dark.
Each laugh echoes, a fleeting sound,
Life's humor lost, yet still profound.

The stage is set, the audience waits,
For witty quips and open gates.
But silence falls, the punchline flies,
And in the stillness, humor sighs.

Yet every stumble brings a cheer,
In comic leaps, we face our fear.
Though punchlines flee without a trace,
We'll chase the smiles in this wild race.

The Absurdity of Everyday Clowns

In morning rush, the coffee spills,
As waiting lines ignite our thrills.
We juggle tasks, the chaos grows,
Masked as clowns in life's grand show.

A honk, a roar, an awkward slip,
In this circus, we laugh and trip.
Life's antics, painted bright and bold,
In every jest, a tale unfolds.

We wear our silliness like a crown,
With frowns and smiles that spin around.
Everyday jesters, lost in play,
Finding joy in the disarray.

Through ups and downs, our laughter streams,
In this absurdity, we chase our dreams.
For every clown, there's joy to seek,
In the mundane, the laughs peak.

Comedy's Twisted Grin

Laughter echoes in the hall,
But who can hear the silent call?
Jokes fly by like birds at dawn,
Yet I sit here, feeling drawn.

Punchlines land like falling fruit,
A twist of fate, a funny hoot.
While everyone else, they burst with glee,
I chase the punchline, but where can it be?

Slapstick antics, a prop or two,
The crowd erupts, cheers like a zoo.
Yet deep inside, I hear the sigh,
Is this the punchline, or just a lie?

When humor hits like bricks from skies,
I laugh along, yet wonder why.
The world spins madly, full of jest,
And here I am, a bemused guest.

The Pantomime of a Half-Hearted Smile

A wink and nudge, the act begins,
With clumsy dancers in oversized skins.
Each step a fumble, a graceful fall,
Who really knows if they'll stand tall?

The jesters prance, a curious sight,
Beneath the laughs, there's something tight.
Fading smiles beneath the paint,
Life's a hoot, yet feels quaint.

Witty banter laced with doubt,
The crowd roars loud, but I'm left out.
The curtain falls; they juggle fears,
And all I gather are sneers and cheers.

With each strange grin, a silent plea,
Is this the humor meant for me?
A backstage clown with no applause,
Just grasping for meaning, lost in the cause.

Shadows of Sarcasm

In corners dark, where shadows creep,
Sarcasm stirs while others sleep.
A wink, a nod, an inside joke,
While I stand there, the awkward bloke.

They dance around with clever quips,
While I just sip from empty sips.
The timing's sharp, the laughter's grand,
Yet I just wander, out of hand.

Each joke a riddle wrapped in snare,
I laugh along, yet feel the glare.
The punchline's lost like socks in wash,
As jesters play, I reckon posh.

A bated breath for what's to come,
A metaphor for feeling dumb.
In the gallery of laughter's spree,
A solo act, just not for me.

The Farce Behind Closed Doors

Behind the curtain, chaos reigns,
With painted smiles and masked refrains.
Each giggle hides a quieter tale,
A story soaked in salty ale.

Whispers echo through the night,
As shadowed figures share their fright.
Beneath the jest, a somber dome,
The laughter fades, not quite at home.

With every tickle, knives grow sharp,
Each jest strikes true, a silent harp.
While others chuckle, I stand aloof,
In a comedy where truth feels spoofed.

The audience rises for the encore fun,
Yet I'm still lost, a previous pun.
Underneath the jest, I search for core,
In life's grand play, I've missed the score.

Chortles from the Cosmos

Stars giggle in the night,
Planets spin in pure delight.
Laughter echoes through the space,
Leaving us with a puzzled face.

The moon winks with a sly grin,
As we stumble trying to fit in.
Galaxies burst with comedic flair,
While we trip over life, unaware.

Time tickles us with its punchline,
Moments fleeting, yet they shine.
We dance in quirks, a cosmic jest,
Finding humor in an unseen quest.

So here we float in this cosmic pool,
Laughing at fate, isn't it cruel?
With every chuckle, we play our part,
In this universe, a funny heart.

Silenced by a Double Entendre

Whispers linger in the air,
Puns dancing without a care.
Words double back, then trip and fall,
Leaving us grinning at it all.

Inside jokes without the frame,
Meanings twist and shift the game.
A punchline hidden in plain sight,
As we chuckle well into the night.

The irony plays peek-a-boo,
Life's layered humor feels so true.
With every misstep, we stumble more,
Each twist and turn opens a door.

So let's raise a glass of silly cheer,
To all the misunderstandings here.
In the grand jest, we play the fool,
And laugh, for laughter is the rule.

Hilarity Wrapped in Confusion

In a world that flips and turns,
Where nothing's certain, laughter burns.
We wear our quirks like fashion's bling,
Amidst the chaos, our hearts sing.

Jokes land flat, but spirits rise,
Life's absurdity met with sighs.
Each blunder shapes the tales we tell,
Finding joy in the fumbles as well.

We chase after wisdom, trip on a shoe,
While cracking up at what we thought we knew.
Laughter comes from the baffled mind,
In all the madness, solace we find.

So join the dance of the unaware,
In this circus, shed every care.
For life's a riddle wrapped in a jest,
With laughter, it's truly at its best.

The Sideshow of Existence

Step right up, the show begins,
Life's a circus, full of spins.
Jokers parade in plain sight,
While we juggle dreams every night.

Balloons burst, confetti flies,
We navigate with wide, surprised eyes.
Every mishap, a twist of fate,
In this grand act, we simply wait.

Clowns paint smiles with every leap,
While we collect memories to keep.
The tightrope walker wobbles and sways,
Life's comedy in so many ways.

So grab a seat and embrace the fun,
In this sideshow, we share the pun.
With laughter as our guiding light,
We revel in this wondrous flight.

The Comedian's Mask

Behind the laughter, a frown hides,
Clowns juggle dreams and jesters ride.
Life's stage is bright, with shadows cast,
A punchline missed, a moment passed.

Each word a tickle, each glance a tease,
Yet wisdom whispers through the breeze.
A slapstick tumble on the floor,
Leaves us giggling, longing for more.

The curtain falls, the laughter fades,
Yet in the echo, hope parades.
We dance on edges, dreams askew,
With every stumble, we find what's true.

With painted smiles and baffled grins,
We play our roles, as fate begins.
The essence lies in every jest,
In silly moments, we are blessed.

Riddles Written in Stardust

Stars wink secrets, wrapped in light,
A riddle here, a quiz in flight.
We search for meaning among the gleam,
While cosmos chuckles at our dream.

Questions dangle like fruit from trees,
Each answer slips, like whispers, free.
The night sky teems with playful lore,
As truths evade, we crave for more.

A comet flashes, a grin so wide,
While dancers trip, in joy they hide.
In cosmic games, we spin and sway,
Chasing laughter, come what may.

In stardust riddles, we find our way,
The universe laughs at our ballet.
So let's embrace the jester's part,
For humor shines within the heart.

Jests of the Unseen Hand

Life's little pranks, no one can see,
Invisible hands caress the spree.
Through twists and turns, we dance in jest,
With fate's own whims, we're ever blessed.

A fortune cookie's cryptic claim,
Yet destiny giggles, plays the game.
In the jigsaw puzzle, pieces stray,
As laughter echoes, come what may.

With every stumble, there's a cheer,
The universe whispers, "Have no fear."
Through chaos and jest, we'll find the song,
A symphony sweet where we belong.

So tip the hat to chance and thrill,
For in its madness, dreams fulfill.
A punchline waiting at each bend,
In giggles and glee, our lives transcend.

Ironies in Everyday Moments

Mismatched socks tell tales untold,
Of silly secrets from days of old.
Coffee spills on plans divine,
While laughter dances on the line.

A cat on a mat, ruling with flair,
While dinner burns, filling the air.
Moments collide, a jester's flight,
In everyday chaos, we find delight.

The mirror cracks, reflections bend,
Yet every flaw is just a trend.
A stumble here, a slip there,
In life's grand joke, we're debonair.

So raise a glass to quirks that shine,
In ironies found, our hearts align.
For every mishap, there's joy to seek,
In absurdity's grasp, we find our peak.

Laughter in Empty Rooms

Whispers dance in silence, loud,
A tickle in the absence, proud.
The echo rolls, a playful hum,
In corners where the stillness comes.

Shadows stretch with cheeky grin,
While cats plot mischief with a spin.
The clock can't keep up with the jest,
Tickles found in every chest.

So here we sit, no problems, none,
Balloons and bubbles, just for fun.
Life's punchline hidden deep in gloom,
Laughter blooms in empty rooms.

The Trickster's Unspoken Rule

A wink exchanged when dusk is near,
Secrets draped in laughter's cheer.
The jester's hat, a crown of dreams,
Wisdom wrapped in playful schemes.

Pass the pie, watch it fly,
Splat! A cream-filled alibi.
In jest, we find our truest face,
With every laugh, we claim our space.

Pranks concealed in serious tides,
Sail through life with jokester rides.
When truth is found in playful shrouds,
The trickster's joy amidst the crowds.

Echoes of a Cosmic Chuckle

Stars wink down with a knowing glance,
Galaxies whirl in a cosmic dance.
Laughter spills from the moonlit cheek,
While planets spin in jest and peek.

Comets dash with joking grace,
In the void, a merry race.
The universe chuckles, a gentle tease,
In every twist, in every breeze.

Black holes hide the punchline's weight,
A timeless riddle that won't abate.
Seek the humor in stellar strikes,
As laughter echoes through cosmic hikes.

The Riddle of a Sore Joke

A riddle wrapped in sarcasm's song,
Makes the wise feel a bit wrong.
When laughter pierces through the thick,
The sore joke lands, a perfect trick.

Fingers crossed, we play along,
In stumbles where the weak are strong.
Knees buckle at a tale retold,
As giggles slip, both shy and bold.

Truth hides behind a joker's mask,
Reveal the punchline, dare to ask.
In every jest, we find the light,
The riddle's laughter, a delightful sight.

The Spectacle of Everyday Farce.

Life spins in circles, oh what a ride,
People clowning, side by side.
Bananas on sidewalks, a slip and a fall,
Everyone's laughing, but I'm lost in it all.

Socks mismatched, who set this trend?
Coffee spills, my trusty friend.
I wear my grin like a well-worn coat,
But the punchline's elusive, just like a goat.

Birds chirping tunes, off key they sing,
Dancing on rooftops, what joy they bring.
A world of quirks, a carnival spree,
I'm just the audience, sipping my tea.

As life unfolds with its quirky flair,
I chuckle quietly, gasping for air.
In the circus of fate, I'm front-row, it seems,
Yet the act's still unfolding, or are they all dreams?

The Punchline is Missing

Walking a tightrope, a balancing feat,
What's the joke? A riddle, a treat?
Faces around me burst into glee,
But I'm stuck on the setup, not sure what to see.

Traffic lights blinking, red, yellow, green,
I'm caught in the middle, not sure what they mean.
People honking and shouting with cheer,
I scratch my head, wish I knew why they're here.

Dinner served cold, the cat steals a bite,
The chef is a clown, but it's not quite right.
With forks like microphones, we play our part,
But the humor escapes me, a comedy heart.

On benches we gather, swapping the tales,
Of slip-ups and stumbles, like wayward snails.
In a world full of laughter, I'm a curious sprite,
Waiting for the punchline, still lost in the night.

Laughing in the Shadows

Shadows dance lightly, caught in the glow,
Laughter flickers softly, secrets we know.
Jesters are hiding behind every door,
Yet their laughter rings true, I beg for more.

Tickle my senses, oh mischievous fate,
With puns on the wind, I can hardly wait.
The world spins in jest, a riddle of care,
While I stand bemused, gasping for air.

Birds burst into giggles, as I walk on by,
While clouds in their wisdom, just wink and sigh.
I stumble through moments, collecting the glee,
But jokes fly right past me, a blurred memory.

In this whimsical dance, I'll continue to grin,
For laughter's a language that pulls me right in.
Though shadows may whisper, my heart's growing light,
In the wonder of jest, I'll stumble through night.

A Mockingbird's Serenade

Listen, the mockingbird's singing away,
Plucking at tunes that will brighten the day.
With each playful chirp, the world feels more bright,
Yet I sit here wondering, is this my spotlight?

Silly little things, like socks on the cat,
Life seems to bubble, like a bubbly spat.
Friends share a chuckle, secrets to trade,
While I'm in the corner, where shadows invade.

Laughter erupts, like popcorn from pots,
But here I remain, counting all the knots.
In this comedy show, I'm lost in the twist,
Searching for stories that hardly exist.

As the mockingbird dances, its rhythm so sweet,
I'll join in the chorus, my heart skips a beat.
For in all the mayhem, there's joy to behold,
In the crooked simplicity, life's tales are told.

Wiping My Tears with a Smile

In a world of rubber chickens,
I stroll with a grin so wide,
As banana peels slip my reason,
I revel in the slapstick tide.

Confetti clouds rain down in jest,
The punchlines trip and fall,
While I'm caught in a clumsy fest,
Am I missing the main hall?

Laughter bubbles up like soda,
Yet I'm stuck with a seltzer spritz,
Life's a party, but my quota,
Is a jest lost in the hits.

I wear a smile, the joker's guise,
In this circus, I play the fool,
With every twist, there's more surprise,
I chuckle in the spinning stool.

Absurdity's Reluctant Partner

The clock strikes thirteen, I check again,
It must be broken, a cosmic joke,
With every tick, the chaos reigns,
As logic sleeps, the nonsense woke.

A cat walks by in men's attire,
With sunglasses on, it steals the show,
I scratch my head, can it inspire?
Absurdity's here, with nowhere to go.

The universe trips on its own shoelace,
And gravity laughs at my fallen pride,
I'm the dancer in a clumsy space,
While the universe takes me for a ride.

With a dance of shadows and bits of light,
I embrace the quirk with open arms,
In this waltz of oddities, I find delight,
For absurdity charms with silly charms.

Tales of a Silent Stand-Up

Here I stand, my mic is dead,
The audience waits, their faces blank,
I mime my jokes, an unseen thread,
In this comedy, I'm a prank.

Laughter echoes in my mind's own hall,
But here I am, lost in a reel,
I juggle thoughts but never recall,
The punchline that got lost in the deal.

The spotlight slices through my doubt,
Yet silence is my only friend,
With each hand gesture, I'm left to shout,
Did laughter die or just pretend?

A bubble bursts—my joke went flat,
And crickets chirp a solemn tune,
Perhaps a chair, I'll play the brat,
In this farce, I'm the afternoon.

The Unfunny Punchline

I step up to the great big stage,
With nerves that twist like a pretzel knot,
But life throws pies with little gauge,
The punchline lands with a silly plot.

With banana skins and rubber frogs,
I trip around, a graceful fall,
Yet every chuckle feels like fogs,
As humor misses, one and all.

A bird in a tux takes center bend,
As I read the room, it's all in vain,
With every wobble, I'm bound to offend,
Is the world just teasing my own pain?

In the end, I raise a toast to fate,
To unseen jesters and laughs unspent,
For every punch that may hesitate,
Leaves me smiling and time well spent.

When Reality Plays the Fool

Each morning greets with socks that don't match,
The sun yawns wide, then sets in a scratch.
A cat in a hat and a dog in a tie,
Who wrote this script, and who asked them to try?

Juggling dreams with a pie in the face,
Life throws a curveball, it's all out of place.
I smile through chaos, a grin stuck like glue,
In this circus of madness, what else can we do?

Birds tweet gossip about life on the ground,
While I'm here laughing, just spinning around.
With every slip, every fall, every laugh,
I'm left wondering if this is the path.

Clowns in the corner, they jump and they play,
Mischief and mayhem steal worries away.
So I twirl with delight in this topsy-turvy spree,
For if life's a joke, it's a fun one for me.

The Cosmic Prank Call

Picked up a phone, but it's not what it seems,
A voice cracks through, filled with laughter and dreams.
"Did you really think it'd all go your way?"
The universe chuckles, like kids at a play.

Light bulbs flicker with each joke they tell,
I turn to my friend, we're under a spell.
With cosmic punchlines that rattle our bones,
Even the planets are talking in tones.

A black hole winks, stars wink back in delight,
Meteor showers have us laughing all night.
The comet zooms by, what a marvelous thrill,
I just hope the punchline's not lacking in skill.

As we ponder the chaos of this grand prank,
We roll in our seats, feeling light as a tank.
In this cosmic theater, we're all players too,
With smiles wide open, when the joke's on you.

Life's Comic Strip Unraveled

With every panel, a fumble, a fall,
Life draws us in like a tapestry small.
Where bubbles burst with each overblown dream,
In a world made of pixels, we giggle and gleam.

The hero trips over a banana peel,
A twist of fate makes us all want to squeal.
Every frame bursting, with laughter, it's true,
When punchlines collide, we don't know what to do.

Pies fly through air like swift little darts,
Comedians prancing with clowns and their smarts.
Yet somehow amidst all the slapstick and cheer,
We find bits of wisdom lurking quite near.

So let's turn the page and rewrite the plot,
With crayons and giggles, let's give it a shot.
For in every misstep, every silly quirk,
Lies the joy of the journey, so come, let's lurk.

In the Theater of Absurdity

Curtains rise slowly, and what do we see?
A penguin in slippers spins wild with glee.
The audience chuckles, they're all in on fun,
As llamas and mimes dance around in the sun.

Each act that unfolds is a riotous theme,
With plot twists that echo like a ridiculous dream.
The waiter's on roller skates, serving blue soup,
While elephants juggle in one wacky loop.

In a world full of nonsense, I sit in my chair,
A laugh in the air and absurd everywhere.
Fish don't read scripts, no, they swim with their grace,
In the grand theater, I embrace the strange space.

So take off your hat, for a moment, just smile,
Life's not about answers or making a trial.
It's a jester's delight in a curious play,
In this theater of life, let's frolic away.

When Life Pulls a Prank

The toaster burns my breakfast toast,
As if it knows I needed toast the most.
The dog steals my socks, oh what a game,
In this circus of life, who's truly to blame?

My plans get tangled like yarn in a mess,
Each day feels like an odd sitcom express.
I trip on my thoughts, they dance and they glide,
In this laughable act, there's nowhere to hide.

The traffic lights flash a quirky show,
Turning red just when it's my turn to go.
Spilled coffee on my shirt, an artist's touch,
Life's comedic timing, oh, it's just too much!

Yet through all the chaos, I grin and I jest,
For hidden in folly, there's humor, the best.
Embracing the quirks, come what may,
In this playful sketch, I long to stay.

The Farce of Expectations

I wake with a goal, goals shiny and bright,
Yet every single plan seems to take flight.
The coffee is cold, my toast is a flop,
Reality laughs as it gives me a chop.

I aim for the stars but hit clouds of fluff,
Expectations soar, but life says, 'Enough!'
In my mind's grand parade, I trip on the way,
The universe winks, 'Let's play today!'

Like scripts on a stage that flop with no sound,
I fumble my lines; laughter's all around.
Each twist and each turn is a comic delight,
In this grand theater, I'm the clown in sight.

So I wear my mishaps like badges of glee,
Finding joy in the chaos, just let it be.
For life's grand illusion is best when it's jest,
In this wonderfully foolish, absurd little quest.

Mirthful Moments in Mundanity

In the still of the morning, with cereal spills,
I sip on my coffee and plow through the thrills.
The cat knocks a vase, it shatters with flair,
As if to announce that chaos is there!

Doing laundry feels like a circus parade,
With socks that play hide-and-seek in the shade.
The dust bunnies leap, throw a dance in the air,
I laugh at the chaos that lives everywhere.

Each trip to the store seems a fine gag reel,
As prices inflate like a comedic wheel.
I leave with more snacks than I ever planned,
Life pokes fun at me, isn't it grand?

The mundane's absurdity brings light to my day,
In the humor of life, I laugh and I sway.
For every small slip, there's joy to be found,
In this lovely lunacy, I'm snugly unbound.

Echoes of the Uninvited Jest

From the office cubicle to the kitchen sink,
Each moment of seriousness starts to shrink.
With knock-knock jokes that linger like air,
Life takes a bow, and I can't help but stare.

Unexpected punchlines in mundane tasks,
With surprises unfolding, just look and you'll bask.
Like shoes on the wrong feet, I waddle around,
In a world full of whimsy, foolishness found.

Conversations turn quirky, like a child's bold dream,
With laughter that sparkles, a delightful theme.
The universe chuckles; I'm part of the scene,
A marionette dancing, oh isn't it keen?

So I raise a toast to the jokes yet untold,
For moments unplanned are treasures of gold.
In every odd quirk, I find joy and jest,
Embracing the whimsy, I'm feeling quite blessed.

The Unseen Hand of Humor

In the circus of fate we play,
The elephants always steal the show.
Clowns with balloons lead the way,
While wise men stand and bow low.

Life's pranks, they dance in disguise,
Juggling dreams behind closed eyes.
Every twist, a surprise,
With punchlines hidden in the skies.

When fortune spins her silly wheel,
The cat and mouse waltz in the reel.
Waiting for turns that never feel,
Like logic's lost charm, a surreal deal.

A grin stretches wide on my face,
As I tumble through this silly place.
With laughter, I try to keep pace,
In a world that's learned to embrace the grace.

Laughter in the Void

In shadows where giggles reside,
The echoes of foolishness collide.
Dancing on edges, I can't decide,
If I'm lost or just taken for a ride.

Each moment a punchline, a flicker of fate,
With humor that teases like a first date.
Silly things happen, don't hesitate,
Laughing at choices while I await.

A tumble and slip, then an invisible hand,
Guides my missteps, though I don't understand.
Life's quirky script poorly planned,
Yet somehow, it's written, grand and unplanned.

From the abyss, giggles emerge,
Lost in a world where snickers surge.
In an expanse where no thoughts converge,
I find joy where the shadows submerge.

Who's Laughing Now?

On the stage of mischief stands a clown,
With shoes too big for this weary town.
He trips and falls, wearing a frown,
Yet the whole world erupts in a sound.

Amid the chaos, wisdom plays hide,
In silliness wrapped tight inside.
All the norms left out to bide,
As laughter escapes, we cannot divide.

With every mishap, the truth unbends,
Those who mock are the first to depend.
A slapstick moment that never ends,
Karma jokes are the real trend!

In the end, who's laughing now?
The jesters with a satirical vow.
While somber faces take a bow,
It's joy that conquers; let me show you how.

Eclipsed by a Laugh Track

Underneath the shining light,
A laugh track masks the dark of night.
I stand in silence, what a sight,
As the punchlines slip out of sight.

In sitcom scenes, the humor flows,
But here reality often slows.
The scripted smiles fade like crows,
While laughter blooms where nobody knows.

In every folly, a lesson sneaks,
Wit plays hide and seek for weeks.
With irony, life coyly peaks,
Giggling softly, it rarely speaks.

So let's embrace the hidden jest,
The cosmic giggle is the best.
As I take this unplanned quest,
In laughter's embrace, I find my rest.

A Clown's Existential Crisis

In a world of bright balloons,
I trip on my oversized shoes.
A painted grin concealing woes,
The mirrors don't reflect the blues.

The audience laughs, a raucous cheer,
While I juggle doubts, full of fear.
Each honk resounds with hidden pain,
Is this joy or just a game?

The pie in the face feels surreal,
As I question what's truly real.
With slapstick falling from my hand,
I ponder jokes I cannot stand.

Underneath the bright marquee,
Who am I — just a fool, not free?
The circus spins, a dizzy tale,
As I search for truth in every fail.

The Laughter That Fades

Echoes of laughter fill the air,
But inside my heart, a vacant stare.
Once, joy danced like a feathered kite,
Now shadows creep with fading light.

The punchline lands, but where's the thrill?
Each chuckle masks a deeper chill.
With painted cheeks and a jolly mask,
I ponder hard on a daunting task.

The jokes grow stale, like bread on a shelf,
Each grin a chore I must compel.
In this carnival of wit and jest,
Am I a superb fool or just the jest?

Life's a riddle wrapped in a wink,
Just when you laugh, you start to think.
The mirth that once was bright and bold,
Now feels like tales that have grown old.

Dissonance in a Comic Dance

Twisting bodies, a clumsy sway,
The beat is off, we laugh away.
When did the rhythm break in two?
I step on toes, not meaning to.

A chuckle shared, but no one's keen,
To join the dance, so terribly mean.
This cacophony of joy and dread,
Behind the giggles, unease spread.

Carousel spins, but I am still,
Trying to find my own lost thrill.
The funny faces, the silly hats,
They hide the strains from where I sat.

In this ballet of mock delight,
I search for truth in the absurd fight.
Each twirl a question, each leap a sigh,
In this dance of fools, I wonder why.

Giggles at the Edge of Reality

At the brink of another jest,
Reality slaps me in the chest.
I giggle softly, a nervous sound,
While cosmic laughter spins around.

Why's the banana always in sight,
When I'm pondering the meaning of night?
A slip, a slide, a merry fall,
In this carnival, I trip, I stall.

The juxtaposition of grim and glee,
Leaves me questioning, could it be we?
Falling, tumbling, through a funhouse door,
An echo of laughter, forevermore.

In the absurdity, I find my place,
Grinning broadly in the wild race.
At the edge of real and surreal strife,
I find my joy in this twisted life.

A Jest on the Edge of Reason

They tell me laughter heals the soul,
As I slip on a banana peel, oh what a toll.
The universe chuckles, a cosmic giggle,
While I just stand there, a clueless wiggle.

With punchlines missed and winks undone,
I'm floating on jokes like I'm the only one.
The humor's a riddle, a maze without maps,
I chase after laughter but fall into traps.

The jesters laugh hard, their eyes full of cheer,
While I fumble for puns, it's all cringe, I fear.
A clown with no audience, the spotlight is bare,
Yet I perform for the echoes that fill up the air.

In shadows they snicker, the wisecrack elite,
While I scratch my head, searching for a beat.
But is it their jest or my clueless refrain?
Ah well, let's toast to the absurdity of pain.

Smiles that Conceal Whispers

Beneath the grin, secrets hide tight,
A chuckle disguises the battle of night.
I walk through a jest that flies overhead,
While I'm left in the ruins of all that I've said.

Every laugh is a puzzle I can't seem to solve,
Like a jigsaw of chaos that won't evolve.
They crack up at chaos, I'm left in confusion,
The punchline's a riddle, a constant illusion.

A wink and a nudge, they read from the script,
While I'm lost in their humor, my own tale eclipsed.
Oh, what's there hidden in whimsy's embrace?
A world full of giggles, a comical space.

I wear my delight like an ill-fitting mask,
While their roars of laughter grow louder, they bask.
Yet here I stand, with a grin painted wide,
Hoping one day I'll share in their ride.

The Unread Script of Existence

The lines were written, but I left them alone,
While the others recite, I am doomed to atone.
With every missed cue, a silent gasp breaks,
As they roll on the floor, my heart just aches.

The stage is alive with laughter and cheers,
While I stand in the dark, dodging my fears.
An unwritten script, I fumble my role,
While the punchlines escape me, out of control.

The humor a melody, I can't seem to hum,
I dance to the silence, a lone drumming bum.
Each chuckle a wave I'm pushed far from shore,
As their joy becomes thunder, I'm left wanting more.

But life carries on, a jest from afar,
With comedy swirling, a cosmic bazaar.
Though I'm not the star of this well-timed parade,
I'll join in the mirth, at least I have strayed.

Jokes That Fall Flat

I tried to tell a joke, it hit the ground hard,
Like my hopes of laughter, left bruised and scarred.
The timing was off, the audience yawned,
An awkward silence downstream, full of ponds.

A pun that once sparkled, tarnished with age,
Left me in stitches, stuck in a cage.
I wander through punchlines, misplaced and grim,
A court jester searching for the humor within.

The laughter around me is a code I can't crack,
While I'm busy rehearsing my ill-fated act.
Yet my fumble grows lighter, a sweet bundle of grace,
As I slip on my comebacks, a clown in the race.

So here's to the missings, the flops that we bring,
That turn into treasures as we dance and we sing.
For the world may be laughing, and I fall in the fray,
But in my own odd way, I join in the play.

The Unscripted Performance

The stage is set, but where's the script?
Lost in laughter, every plan flipped.
Actors trip on lines so absurd,
While the audience giggles, not a word.

The props are here, yet nothing's right,
A banana peel brings comedic fright.
We dance through chaos, a scripted mess,
In this grand show, who needs success?

With confetti falling from skies unknown,
We juggle dreams, yet feel alone.
Each punchline lands, but fades away,
In this unscripted play, we sway.

So laugh with me, as we fumble on,
In this wild act, we'll still have fun.
The curtains close, but the joy remains,
In this cosmic farce, nothing's in chains.

Joking with Destiny

I asked fate for a little grace,
It just responded with a smiling face.
Cards are shuffled, my luck's a bluff,
Jokes spun out, but never enough.

Life tosses quips like a frisbee's flight,
Chasing them down, it's quite the sight.
Each twist and turn, a chuckle erupts,
While I ponder if I'm the one who corrupts.

Destiny winks with a playful tease,
Whispers of chaos carried on the breeze.
We dance along this unpredictable line,
With every misstep, we laugh and shine.

So let's toast to the cosmic giggle,
In this crazy ride, we must wriggle.
For even in sorrow, humor's a must,
In this game of jest, in laughter we trust.

Satirical Whirlwinds

Round and round, the whirlwind spins,
A tempest of folly, where no one wins.
Life throws pies in a comical quest,
But we just laugh, 'cause jest is the best.

With every gust, a new joke flies,
Tickling ribs, beneath the skies.
As we tumble through absurdity's sway,
There's laughter within the disarray.

The clock ticks slowly, time stands still,
While we line up for more of this thrill.
Chasing the clouds, we skip and hop,
In this cyclone of laughter, we'll never stop.

So grab your hats, hold on real tight,
For in this maelstrom, we find our light.
And when the storm finally lets go,
We stand in puddles of comic woe.

Punchlines in the Silence

In quiet moments, the punchlines bloom,
Little whispers that chase away gloom.
A wink from a stranger, a nudge from fate,
Life's best humor waits, can't be late.

Between the chaos, a chuckle sneaks,
Hiding in shadows, it softly peaks.
In the stillness, a giggle takes flight,
Jokes wrapped in silence, a pure delight.

The world keeps spinning, mismatched shoes,
With every step, there's always a muse.
To laugh at the quiet, with friends by my side,
In this jest of existence, we take in stride.

When laughter erupts in the hush of night,
We dance with silliness, hearts feeling light.
So listen closely, the world has its say,
In punchlines of silence, we find our way.

The Universe's Hidden Quips

Stars twinkle like they've got a joke,
A cosmic giggle through the smoke.
Planets dance in a silly parade,
While I'm left grinning, slightly dismayed.

Comets zoom past, with a wink and a grin,
They laugh at the chaos, as if it's a win.
I search for the punchline, lost in the night,
But all I find is the oddest delight.

Galaxies spiral, with secrets untold,
While I'm just here, feeling somewhat cold.
Nebulae chuckle, as I scratch my head,
Wondering about the things left unsaid.

Maybe it's me, I'm missing the clue,
The universe chuckles, what's new?
Perhaps I should laugh at the cosmic jest,
And find joy in the chaos, like all the rest.

When the Clowns Came to Town

The clowns marched in, all colors and cheer,
With big red noses and silly beer.
They juggled my worries, tossed them around,
Turning my frown into sounds profound.

With shoes too big and laughter galore,
They tripped over dreams, fell down on the floor.
I watched in awe as they painted the sky,
With squirting flowers and pies flying high.

While I sipped my soda, they danced in delight,
Twisting and turning, a colorful sight.
In the midst of their antics, I found a grin,
Life's just a circus, where we all fit in.

So, when clowns came in, they turned my frown,
Into a giggle, a joy I could crown.
Life may be wild, but with laughter it glows,
Like jester's hat and a nose that just grows.

Serenade of Misunderstandings

I asked for a cake, they gave me a pie,
I laughed and I sighed, thought I might cry.
Misunderstandings, oh what a treat,
Like socks with sandals, a mix-up so sweet.

I tried to fit in, but stepped on a duck,
It quacked with surprise, oh what bad luck!
Yet here I am, in a world so absurd,
Finding the humor in all that I've heard.

Conversations tangled like spaghetti at night,
Each word a noodle, just not quite right.
But laughter erupts like a breath of fresh air,
In this serenade, we lighten the wear.

So let's toast to the gaffes, the slips, and the falls,
To the joy found in life's comical brawls.
For in every mishap, there's fun to behold,
A story worth sharing, a joke to be told.

Smiles Behind the Curtain

Behind the curtain, the jesters all grin,
Hiding their chuckles, the fun's about to begin.
Life's a play, with scripts gone awry,
Where laughter is scattered like stars in the sky.

The stage is set with props made of dreams,
A little confusion, but bursting at seams.
Foot in the mouth, oh what a delight,
In the chaos of life, we find our insight.

Every mishap's a treasure, a gem of its own,
With giggles and snorts, we've brightly outgrown.
As the world spins round, in its dizzying whirl,
I'll dance with the clowns, watch the feathers unfurl.

So pull back the curtain, let laughter take flight,
For smiles are the magic that brightens the night.
In the theater of life, we're all in the act,
Finding joy in the funny, that's a simple fact.

www.ingramcontent.com/pod-product-compliance
Lightning Source LLC
Chambersburg PA
CBHW071853160426
43209CB00003B/541